GOOD DOG, BAD DOG:
THE GOLDEN BONE

This is for Mum and Dad, with love.

With thanks to Joel Stewart, Emma Bonsall,
Portia Rosenberg, Woodrow Phoenix and Pam Smy.

Enormous extra special thanks
to Faz and to Lovely Ben Sharpe.

Good Dog Bad Dog: The Golden Bone
is a
DAVID FICKLING BOOK

First published in Great Britain in 2010 as
GOOD DOG BAD DOG: BOOK 1 (DFC LIBRARY)
by David Fickling Books, an imprint of The Random House Group

This new edition published in 2017 by
David Fickling Books,
31 Beaumont Street,
Oxford, OX1 2NP

www.davidficklingbooks.com

GOOD DOG, BAD DOG:
THE GOLDEN BONE

By Dave Shelton

The Golden Bone of Alexandria
coloured by Faz Choudhury

DOG MEETS DOG

The name's Bergman.

Kirk Bergman.

But you can call me "Detective".

As in "Please don't shoot, Detective. I'll come quietly".

Hold it right there, Dupree!

Hah!

Well now, Bergman, what do you think ...

... if I jump, will I make it?

I don't know. But if you try I'll shoot you.

Hey, take it easy, Detective, I'm only kidding.

I'll come quietly.

Good decision. Now get down off that wall. We don't want any nasty...

... accidents.

ERK!

trip

WAAAAH!

Oof!

Meanwhile, down on the ground...

Excuse me, officer...

I'm Detective McBoo. I was meant to meet Detective Bergman at HQ, but I missed him. Is he here?

Oh, hello, Sir. Yes, Detective Bergman is in pursuit of a suspect in the McCay Building over there.

Oh yes? Do you think he'll be long?

Um, difficult to say, Sir. You'd better see for yourself.

Oh deary me!

Crikey! I'd better go and help out. You stay here. And radio for an ambulance.

Just in case.

James "Wheels" Dupree, I am arresting you on suspicion of a whole bunch of bad stuff...

You have the right to remain silent. And I suggest you do. I'm in no mood to chat.

Whatever you say, Bergman, just don't let go of my leg!

LIFT OUT OF ORDER

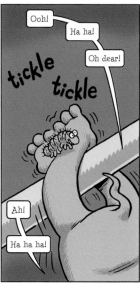

I tell ya, Bergman, I was the other side of town visiting my granny.

Quit wasting my time, Dupree! I've got better things to do than listen to your fairy stories!

We know you drove the car for the Bagel Street robbery. Now tell me who the stick-up guy was and I'll go easy on you.

Ah, can it, Bergman! You've got nothing on me and we both know it. Stop being such a dummy, let me go and you can go chase some pigeons or somethin'.

Don't you **ever** call me a dummy, Wheels Dupree!

Erk!

I'll tear your tail off and shove it up—

Eek!

Tea and cake, Mr Dupree?

Oh, so it's the old good cop/bad cop routine, is it? Can't you chumps be a bit more original?

I don't know what you mean. Now be careful, this tea is very ...

... hot.

Oop!

trip

OW! OW!

OW!

Oh, I'm so sorry, Mr Dupree...

WAH!

slip

OOF!

SQUISH!

OW!

Ooooooh!

Okay, okay...

I did the bank job with Gruff Growler, okay? He's holed up in Apartment 13, Longden House.

Now get off me, will ya?

Let's go, partner.

Nice work, McBoo.

9

Longden House.

BARKING 2 WOOF

94,000, 95,000 96,000... Ho boy!

Who's that?

KNOCK KNOCK

POLICE!

Open up, Growler!

Erk!

Luckily, I can make a quick exit down the old fire escape.

EEK!

Hello, Mr Growler, lovely day. Off out for a stroll?

Now, I'm afraid I am going to have to arrest you. I do hope that's okay?

Uh, yeah, sure thing, copper.

Oh good. I do so hate any ...

... unpleasantness.

Oh dear.

Stick 'em up, copper!

THE GOLDEN BONE OF ALEXANDRIA

A burglary? It's an outrage!

Twenty-one years on the force ... murders, kidnappings, bank heists ...

... and they waste my time with a burglary case? It's embarrassing!

Aye, well, it's no ordinary burglary.

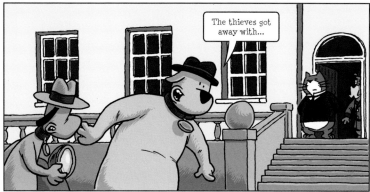

The thieves got away with...

... THE GOLDEN BONE OF ALEXANDRIA!

Sir Garfield Woofington, I presume?

Yes, yes, quite.

So you're the young pups who are going to track down the brigands who've robbed me, eh?

Cardigan, get these fellows some drinks would you?

Certainly, Sir.

Gentlemen?

Bourbon.

No ice.

Banana milk-shake please.

No ice for me either.

The bounders seem to have broken in through the French windows.

Your bourbon, Sir.

Thanks.

So, this golden bone... I guess it's worth a few bucks, huh?

It's utterly priceless!

Forged in solid gold and intricately carved by the greatest craftsmen of the ancient world ...

Your milkshake, Sir.

Yum!

... It was created for Alexander the Great, as a gift to his faithful companion, Ozzy ...

Who's a good boy? Who's a good doggy?

... but was almost immediately lost and remained so for many centuries.

Fetch, boy!

Go on, boy, fetch the bone!

Fetch the expensive bone!

Fetch the really, really expensive bone...

We can only guess at what happened...

Oh dear.

Its later history is hazy but bloody. So many lives were lost in its pursuit that some said the bone was cursed. By the mid-seventeenth century it was lost again and many thought it no more than a myth.

My grandfather learned of the bone's existence in 1931 and immediately knew that he had to make it his own.

He commissioned the famous adventurer Idaho Smith to seek it out. Smith tracked it down to Borneo and brought it back to this country ...

... where it has remained in the Woofington family's possession ... until this morning.

I presume the bone was kept somewhere suitably secure?

Shlluurrp

Burp!

Aye. You can't be too careful.

ching!

Well normally it wouldn't be kept in the house at all.

Usually it stays in the high security vault of Barkly's Bank...

Phew!

...and this replica remains on display here.

But yesterday I had the real bone brought here secretly to show to Lady Agatha Dumfries who was paying a vist.

Coo.

Somehow the thieves knew all about it. They ignored the fake and stole the real bone from the safe...

Cardigan, take down Sir Henry, could you.

Certainly, Sir.

No sign of forced entry. And none of the alarms were triggered. They're clever devils I fear.

It's a professional job all right. Who might have done it?

Hmm...

Oh, now... what's this?

Maybe the Bixley Twins... Or the Lamp Street Gang...

Ooh, a book of matches!

Weird how often that happens!

"The Club Fifi"

Say – isn't that place run by...?

WAH WAH JOHNSON!

That lowdown hound! He won't escape from me this time!

THWACK

Come on, McBoo.

We're going to see a dog about a bone!

So, you've had dealings with this Johnson fellow before?

Yeah.

Bix Beagle and me had connected Johnson to the Rosenberg diamond heist.

We caught the gang and got the diamonds back...

... but when we went to get Johnson he got clean away and we wound up trapped in a burning building.

I lost a pretty good partner that day.

And my favourite hat!

Ooh!

We're there.

stomp!

Eek!

WHUMP!

Oop.

Club Fifi

Ooh, could I get a milkshake please?

Hurry up, McBoo! We haven't got time...

Kirk Bergman! How rude!

Fifi?

Haven't you even got time to buy an old friend a drink?

Fifi LaConfiture
– what's it been?
Seven years?

Honey, it's
been fourteen!

You were singing at the
Bow Wow Club back then.
Now you're working for a
creep like Wah Wah Johnson?

A girl's gotta
work, Sugar.

Well, Fifi, you haven't
changed a bit.

You have.

You got a
new hat.

That reminds me.
I need to see your
boss. He in?

Yeah. He's here.

Through the
back there.

Thanks, Fifi.
Good to see you.

I'll be back to
buy you that
drink sometime.

Sure.

Staff only back here.

Buzz off, copper!

Spud Mulligan! So
you're working for
Wah Wah now, huh?
That figures.

Well you'll step aside
if you know what's
good for you!

Hur!
Am I meant to
be scared of you?

Um, no …
not really …

WHAM!

… but you might want
to be scared of him!

Come on, McBoo.
Come and meet
the most dangerous
dog in the city!

WAH WAH
JOHNSON!

Ah, my old
friend Mr
Bergman.

Come in,
come in…

I've been expecting you.

Well, well...
Kirk Bergman!

So good to see
you again.

And this must be
your new partner...?

Duncan McBoo.
Pleased to meet
you, Mr Johnson.

Charmed.

Hmm ... he's bigger than
the last fellow isn't he?

Sturdy.

Maybe he'll last a
little longer, eh?

GRRRRR!

So, what can I do for you,
gentleman? I'm always
eager to help the police
with their enquiries.

And let's face it,
you need all the
help you can get.

Can it, Johnson!

We know you've got
the Golden Bone!

We found this at the
scene of the crime!

Oh, how
marvellously
quaint.

SLAM!

21

Mr Green, my name's Detective McBoo. I wonder if you could help me?

Shove off, copper!

McBoo, what do you think you're...

Oh!

You really shouldn't be so rude, Mr Green. You might upset someone.

Now, as I was saying...

Eek!

You know, it's amazing how public-spirited people can be if they're just given the right encouragement.

Farley's Bar, over on Wag St. We can be there in fifteen minutes.

SLAM!

Of course, we'll need to go undercover.

Ooh, goody! Dressing up!

9.55 p.m.

Farley's BAR

You know, McBoo, I'm just not sure about these disguises.

Are you kidding? Our own mothers wouldn't know us!

Anyway, we were lucky to find that all-night fancy dress shop at all!

Ooh, there's Wah Wah, in the corner booth there.

And look – coming in the door now ... I'll bet that's the "CC" fellow that he's meeting.

Ahem, so, Uncle Gilbert, how was your trip?

Arr! It was fine.

You were right. He's going over to Wah Wah!

And I'll bet that parcel is the golden bone!

Gasp! Look – it's Cardigan, Sir Garfield's butler!

So, it was an inside job!

The butler did it! Who'd have guessed.

SNAP

We'd better get out of here and call for back-up. This place is swarming with Wah Wah's hoodlums!

Quietly does it.

Don't do anything to draw attention to yourself.

Okay.

Uh oh!

AAARAAAARRGH!

Oh!

Oh!

Oh!

Oh dear!

I think I just lost us the deposit on the costumes.

Why look – it's your detective friends.

Excellent!

GET THEM, BOYS!

Erk!

26

Before long...

You know, McBoo, that was pretty smart.

Aye. I surprise myself sometimes.

Not that I was worried at all.

No, of course not.

A breath of fresh air, perhaps?

Don't mind if I do.

No atmosphere in this place anyway.

Not so fast, gentlemen.

Spud, Curly – if you'd be so kind?

Oh dear. And just when everything was going so well.

Hello again, Spud. I like what you've done with that eye. It really suits you.

WHAM!

Okay, boys.

Tie them up and bring them along.

And no arguing about who gets to kill them!

sproing

SPLASH!

WAH!

SPLOSH!

Ach!

Awww! What did you have to do that for?

I was having such a lovely dream.

Hah! Don't you worry. You'll—

Hang on a second...

CURLY!

What do I pay you for?

Can't you see I need a box here?

That's better. Er, now where was I?

Um ... "Hah! Don't you worry. You'll—"

Ah yes. Thank you. Ahem...

Don't worry, Detective McBoo, you'll be sleeping again soon enough. You'll be sleeping **for a very long time!**

Ooh, that's no good. I need to get up early in the morning to go and visit my mum.

It's her birthday.

Gah! I didn't really mean you'd be sleeping, you idiot! I meant you'd be **dead!**

Oh. I see.

Well, that's not very nice, is it?

Nice?

It's not meant to be nice! **I'm** not meant to be **nice!**

I'm evil!

I'M AN EVIL GENIUS!

Oops!

WHUMP!

Nice going there, genius!

SHUT UP! SHUT UP!

At least I'm smarter than the pair of you.

Smart enough to steal the Golden Bone. And more importantly ...

... smart enough not to get caught.

Comfortable, Mr Bergman? Ropes not too tight, I hope.

Ah, shaddup!

Ow!

Paf

Well, that hurt, Mr Bergman, but it's the last pain you will ever cause me.

Who would have thought it? All the years you've been such an irritation to me ...

... and in the end all it took to get you out of my fur ...

... all it took to lure you to your doom ...

... was a book of matches!

You set us up?

Of course, my dear boy. I **am** a genius!

Time to go, Boss.

Oh, gentlemen, I'm sorry. It's been so lovely to see you but I have a boat to catch.

A client in Cairo wishes to pay me a great deal of money for the Golden Bone and it would be rude to keep him waiting.

But I'm sure that Spud will take very good care of you for me.

Oh yes. I'll take care of you all right!

Well now, this **is** cosy isn't it?

Alone at last.

And not a soul around for miles.

No one can save you now!

Well actually ...

... there is someone!

Oh yeah? And who's that, exactly? Your fairy godmother?

No, don't be silly.

Bartholomew Quigley will save us.

Get him, Bartholomew!

Meanwhile, just behind McBoo's ear...

What's that?

Cripes! The boss is in trouble!

To the rescue!

Stop trying to kid me, copper. There's no one...

Mmmmmm...

CHOMP!

Tasty!

Uh?

chomp

OW!

chomp

chomp

Didn't know you had fleas, McBoo.

Just the one. We have an arrangement.

Gah!

Ow!

Scratch Scratch

Now ... can you reach my hat?

Your hat? Why...?

Oh, I see.

Nnff!

chomp!

chomp!

Scratch Scratch

Nnnggg!

Raaah!

PAF!

Steady...

Steady...

Got it!

34

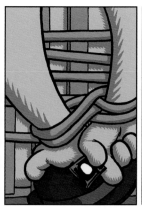

Ooyah!

Rrrr!

Oh! Oh! Oh!

Nearly there...

Ow! Ow! Ow!

SNAP!

Ooooh ... that's better!

Okay, Bartholomew, that's enough now.

Thank you.

Ah, the relief...

Ooooh...

Oh!

WHAM!

CRASH!

Untie me, McBoo! There's no time to lose!

Righto.

Now ...

... let's finish this thing!

35

Come on, McBoo. Wah Wah can't be far ahead of us.

You can't go that fast on legs as short as his.

There's Curly!

Hold it right there, Mulligan!

Boss! It's the cops!

Bergman? Curses! That dog has more lives than a cat!

Curly! Quickly!

Throw down the bone!

Okay, Boss. On three.

One, two ...

... thraaaaah!

OOF!

Nice work, McBoo.

Johnson ...

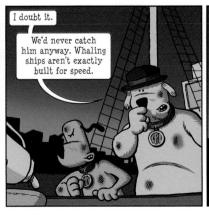

I don't see any harpoons, McBoo. We'll have to improvise.

We need something long, thin and heavy.

We'll call it a draw this time shall we, Bergman?

I don't get the Golden Bone, you don't get to lock me away. Nobody wins.

Still – no hard feelings, eh?

Wrong on every count!

PAF

MISCHIEF

CLANG!

Erk!

flump!

click

Nice shootin' there, cowboy!

Thank you very much.

Pfff

Later...

Well done, Bergman. You've recovered the bone and Wah Wah Johnson is behind bars at last – now that's what I call a good day's work.

Thanks, Chief.

What's that you're saying, Chief?

Oh, just ... Nice collar, McBoo!

What, this old thing?

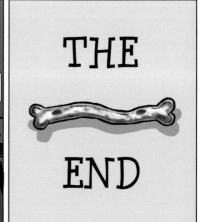

THE

END

THE DOGS' DINNER

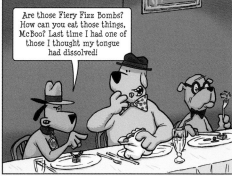

I don't know what the fuss is about. They've never done me any harm.

Oh, apart from that time I went blind...

But that was only for a couple of weeks.

Uh oh! Here come the speeches.

His worship, Mayor Flanagan.

Ladies and gentlemen...

Before we move on to the main course, I'd like to take a moment to introduce our very special chef for this evening ...

... Anton Le Boof!

Sank you, sank you.

TARAN TARA

Yes, it is true. Tonight you are truly privileged to be served the finest dishes in all the world, prepared by moi, the great Anton Le Boof!

Cuisine Magazine's Chef of the Year!

Celebrated inventor of the chocolate sprout!

Three time winner of the Golden Crepe Award!

clap clap clap

clap clap clap

And highly commended for my beetroot chutney by the Neasden Women's Institute!

Yes, tonight your palates will be caressed to exquisite pleasure by the greatest delicacies ...

... prepared by the greatest genius of the culinary arts that the world has ever known!

I sank you.

Do you think there'll be jelly and ice cream for pudding? I like jelly and ice cream.

Later...

I don't need to tell you, Bergman - this looks bad for the department!

A kidnapping right under the noses of our two top dogs!

Don't sweat, Chief, we're working this case hard!

Uniform are taking statements from the guests.

And maybe the lab boys will turn up something from the bullets ...

... or the cake. If there's any left by then!

McBoo, quit eating the evidence, wouldya?!

Oop!

Um, I was just ... investigating it ...

... with my mouth.

You have to be very thorough on a case like this!

We've got our best dogs on this one, Chief. We'll soon turn something up.

That's all very well, Bergman, but what leads do you have right now?

I need fast results on this one or the press will have a field day!

The press! Of course! Now where is ...

... SCOOP BAILEY!

Hold it right there, paperboy!

You got pictures of the whole shebang-bang, didn't you? Hand over the cameras, Scoop!

Aw, geez Louise, Bergman! I coulda won the Puppitzer Prize with those shots!

Aw, I'm weeping for you, Bailey. Those pictures are evidence now!

You'll have to console yourself with the warm glow of having done your duty as a citizen.

Sure, sure...

My editor pays me a bonus when I glow warmly.

You'll be okay, Scoop. Play nice and maybe we'll throw you a bone when we wrap this case up.

Meantime, remind me: what's the name of that restaurant critic at The Post?

47

Later, at the Rover Café...

Daniel Spaniel?

Yes, dear boy ... mmm ... what can I do for you?

Detective Bergman, CPD. This is my colleague, Detective McBoo.

Scoop Bailey told us we might find you here...

Hullo there.

Detectives? How thrilling! Will you join me? I seem to have rather over-ordered again.

No thanks, we already ate and we're on duty.

Um, yes. That's right.

Oh well ... munch ... that is a shame. But tell me ... mmm yum ... how can I help you?

A jumped up burger-flipper, name of Le Boof, got himself kidnapped tonight. You know him?

Oh, how ... nyum ... dreadful! Poor Anton!

But I'm afraid I won't be much help to you. I can vouch for the quality of his marrowbone soufflé but I've only actually met Anton once or twice, and then only very briefly.

Uh huh. But still, perhaps with your connections in the restaurant world you might have an idea of any enemies Le Boof might have...

Enemies?

No, no ... munch ... I've no idea. I'm afraid that the talented Monsieur Le Boof is something of ... gulp ... a mystery.

He arrived as if from nowhere a year ago and took the city by storm with his daring new recipes.

POSH NOSH! Snooty Chef Sensation!

He had a meteoric rise to the top of his profession, rave reviews from all the critics, myself among them ...

... but no scandal, no gossip, no enemies. Perhaps someone from his past but, as I say, his past is a mystery!

I see.

So sorry I can't be more help.

Detective Bergman, Sir!

The lab sent me over with these for you. Said you wanted to see them as soon as possible.

Aha! Scoop's photos. Thanks, Officer Dooley.

No need to worry yourself, Spaniel. As you can see, we have other leads to work on.

Come on, McBoo.

Oh, righto. Bye bye, Mr Spaniel. Lovely to meet you.

A pleasure, dear boy.

CRASH!

SMASH!

ERK!

Oop!

Sorry about that.

Come on, McBoo!

Rover Cafe

I shall have someone attend to the mess at once, Monsieur Spaniel.

Thank you, Marcel.

And could I have another bottle of the St Radegund '24, please.

And the telephone. There's a rather important call I need to make.

Aw, come on, Frank. Jusht one more liddle drinkeroonie.

One lasht one for the road? Whaddyasay?

I say you should go home and sleep it off, Barney. You've had enough.

I'll say when I've had enough, you lousy...

WAAAAFT!

Excuse me, Sir, I'll be needing your stool for important police business.

You just hang around here until you've calmed down a bit.

Milkshake, please, Frank.

You stay out of trouble, McBoo. I'll find—

Why, Kirk Bergman! Second time in seven years you've come here. People will talk!

... Fifi.

You here to buy me that drink, Detective?

Or am I just helping you with your enquiries?

x

Strictly business today, Fifi.

Always is with you, isn't it, Kirk?

You **ever** do anything just for fun?

Fun?

Sure, I tried that once.

Didn't like it!

Anyway, I figured you get a lot of lowlife, no good criminal types passing through this place...

No offence, boys.

None taken.

No, fair point.

Thanks very much.

So I figured you might recognise some of the hoods in these pictures.

Let's see ... Nope ... nope ... uh uh ... no ...

AHA!

Someone you recognise?

Oh yeah, real dangerous-lookin' type!

Not sure they got your best side though, Kirk!

Ah, quit foolin', Fifi! If you can't help me then I'll just...

No, wait! There **is** someone. Here in the background of this one.

I know him!

Well, sure, that's Anton Le Boof. We know that already. But he's the victim. We're kinda more interested in the criminals.

Le Boof? Is that what he's calling himself now?

When I knew him he was fresh out of jail and his name was Jimmy Kibble!

"You're sure?"

"Sure I'm sure!"

"The big floppy hat and the beard are new but that's Jimmy all right!"

"He was running with the Lamp Street Gang for a while."

"He got caught during a hold up. Did a little time in The Pound."

"Last time I saw him he was talking about going straight. Said he'd learned to cook a little in jail."

"Got himself a job at Hopper's Diner. You know it?"

"Hopper's? Sure, over in Muttville."

"McBoo! We're leaving!"

"Righto."

"Thanks, Fifi."

"I'll come back someday soon and buy you that drink I owe you."

"Sure, sure."

"Someday..."

"We're looking for Harry Hopper. He working tonight?"

"Sure, Detective, he's out back in the kitchen."

"You here to arrest him for crimes against my stomach?"

"You can have my burger as evidence."

"RIGHT! THAT'S IT! I'VE HAD ENOUGH!"

"NOW I'M GOING TO KILL YOU!"

Quick, McBoo!

I'M GOING TO KILL YOU!

WAAAAH!

THUNK!

Sorry about that.

I didn't scare you, did I?

I've got a bit of a cockroach problem. I've been after that little monster all week!

Ouch!

Good shot though!

So, anyway, how can I help you, Detectives?

You know a dog name of Jimmy Kibble?

Sure, Jimmy worked here for a while.

He in trouble?

Not with us. But, yeah, he's in trouble. You want to help him?

Help you, you mean?

Well, yes. That too, I suppose.

Aw, go on. We'd be very grateful.

Yeah, that's right.

Maybe even grateful enough not to tell the health department about the state of your kitchen and get you closed down!

No need for that. I'm always happy to help you police dogs.

Let me just check on the customers out front and then I'll answer all your questions.

Hmf!

Darned police hounds are bad for business. Don't they know I need to look after my customers?

All right, then!

Which of you lousy, rotten deadbeats need more coffee?

You know I was only joking, but we really **ought** to report him. This place is **disgusting!**

When do you think he last even bothered to do any washing up?

Three or four days at least, I reckon.

Lucky for me!

Yum ... cake mix!

Mmm ... lemony!

!

Bergman! Hopper made the big cake!

What?

You're sure?

Aye! I don't know much, but I do know about cake!

Right! Let's arrest Hopper and get him down to the station. We'll see what we can get out of him there.

Finally we're—

BANG!

Aaargh!

Dammit!

Tch. As if the service in this place wasn't bad enough already!

Oh, that really is quite inconvenient!

Hopper, quickly, you may not have much time! Who did this to you?

And how did you make the sponge in the cake so light?

Nnnff.

Um...

Can I help you, Detective?

Help me? It's a bit late for that!

You could have helped me by not shooting Harry Hopper!

Um, Bergman ...

Shooting? What do you mean?

Don't play the innocent with me, buddy!

BERGMAN!

I think maybe Mr Hopper wasn't pointing at this gentleman at all.

Look! A bullet hole in the window. The shooter was outside.

Ah! Yes.

Well ... you just watch yourself!

Ahem.

Come on, McBoo!

The shooter will be long gone, but we'll take a look outside for clues.

Hang on a minute, Bergman.

Look at this photo. Hopper, Kibble ... and Daniel Spaniel.

Spaniel said he didn't know anything about LeBoof's past – why did he lie?

I don't know, McBoo. Let's go and ask him!

Righto.

Oh, and somebody call an ambulance will you?

Bye, Mr Hopper. Nice to meet you. Take care.

Groan.

Well, that was all very upsetting!

Shooting!

Police brutality!

False accusations!

And my teaspoon was dirty!

I think, under the circumstances, that I won't leave a tip!

55

Mmmf?

What's...?

Who's...?

A car?

What time...?

Who on earth...?

Oh, no!

Oh, dear!

Oh, no!

Hurry up!

Answer, for heaven's sake!

Oh, thank goodness!

They're here!

Yes, the detectives I told you about.

Very well. But, please, hurry!

CRASH!

Knock, knock!

Hello again, Mr Spaniel.

Um, sorry about the door, Mr Spaniel. I don't know my own strength sometimes!

Really, gentlemen, if you have more questions for me...

Questions?

Sure! Here's one:

"How come you didn't tell us that Anton Le Boof used to be Jimmy Kibble?"

Or here's another:

"Why would you lie to a detective if you had nothing to hide?"

Or how about this one:

"Which is better: free dinners every night at the finest restaurants ..."

"... or prison food?!"

You don't scare me, Detective Bergman.

Shout all you like, I'll not say a word to you without my lawyer present.

Oh, you'll talk, Spaniel...

Oh, go on, Mr Spaniel. I like a good chat.

I'll give you a sweetie!

Good idea, McBoo.

Is it? Really? I always hoped I'd have one someday!

Yes. Let's give Mr Spaniel a sweetie...

I'm sure that with his very delicate, highy refined sense of taste that he'll appreciate your **Vesuvios** even more than you do!

Vesuvios?! Oh, dear Lord!

Come on, Spaniel - open wide!

Please ... don't...

Say "Aah"!

AAAAAARGH!

All right, all right.

I'll talk. Just give me **water!**

That's better. Now spill it, Spaniel!

All right ... glub ... all right!

I knew Kibble, it's true.

I haven't always been a reviewer of fancy restaurants. I had to work my way up from ... humbler esatblishments.

As such I mixed, for a while, with some very shady characters.

I was delighted when my work began to take me to more respectable places and I was able to leave these underworld connections behind.

Or so I thought...

'Ullo, Spaniel, got a proposition for you.

You'll like it ...

... if you know what's good for you.

This dangerous fellow wanted to find Kibble.

I didn't ask why. I didn't wish to know.

As chance would have it, shortly afterwards I visited a new restaurant with a remarkable new chef called...

Anton Le Boof!

Yes. He pretended not to know me. As if the beard and the terrible accent would be enough to fool me.

And you told your gangster pal that Kibble was now Le Boof.

And he sent a cake full of hoods to the Mayor's dinner to snatch him.

So who is he, this gangster?

It's...

Pug Ugly!

Pug Ugly?

Excellent! I've been trying to pin something on him for years.

Come on, McBoo. Let's pay that ugly thug a visit!

Good idea...

We'll give you a lift!

Erk!

'Ere 'e is. Safe and sound.

You're a popular boy, Jimmy. These detectives are concerned for your well-being. Ain't that sweet?

Oh well, that's lovely, Mr Ugly.

If you could just remove his leg irons we'll take Mr Kibble home and say no more about it.

Erk!

Or possibly you'd prefer it if he stayed here?

Chik

Yur.

We went to quite a bit of trouble to find 'im again so I'd like to 'ang on to 'im, ta.

See, I tried to 'ire 'im as my personal chef back when 'e was working for 'Arry 'Opper but 'e turned me down flat and did a bunk.

Bit rude, that. Didn't like it.

Didn't like it at all.

Made me irked.

Awright, Jimmy, back to work now, son.

Luckily, I've got a lot of contacts one way and another.

Fingers in a lot of pies: bars, theatres, restaurants, newspapers...

I can find out most things if I set my mind to it.

So we found Jimmy.

And we asked 'im again.

And managed to persuade 'im.

I generally do get my way.

So now Jimmy works for me and everybody's 'appy.

Oh yes. So very happy.

So you didn't kidnap Jimmy for a ransom? You went to all this trouble just so you had someone to cook your breakfast?

Most important meal of the day! And let me tell you — nobody ...

... NOBODY ...

... makes beans on toast like this boy!

Aah! Luvverly!

Beans on toast? Mmm ... yum!

Now if you just bear with me, gents ... SNURF!

... then just as soon as I'm done ... SLURP!

URP!

... we can get on with the business at hand.

I do so hate killing nosy coppers on an empty stomach!

See — that's the beauty of owning a scrapyard: it's so convenient for disposing of unwanted rubbish.

Right then, boys, bung them in that old jalopy...

... so I can lift them with the magnet ...

... and drop them in the crusher!

Lovely!

CRUSHOMATIC 3000

Any thoughts, McBoo?

I wish we'd had breakfast!

THE END

64